101 THINGS® TO DO WITH A
CASSEROLE

101 THINGS® TO DO WITH A
CASSEROLE

STEPHANIE ASHCRAFT
& JANET EYRING

Gibbs Smith

Second Edition
27 26 25 24 23   5 4 3 2 1

First Gibbs Smith edition published in 2005
Second Gibbs Smith edition published May 2023

Published by
Gibbs Smith, Publisher
P.O. Box 667
Layton, Utah 84041

1.800.835.4993 orders
www.gibbs-smith.com

Designed by Ryan Thomann and Renee Bond
Printed and bound in China
Gibbs Smith books are printed on either recycled, 100% post-consumer
waste, FSC-certified papers or on paper produced from sustainable PEFC-
certified forest/controlled wood source. Learn more at www.pefc.org.

The Library of Congress has cataloged the first edition as follows:
Ashcraft, Stephanie.
101 things to do with a casserole / by Stephanie Ashcraft and Janet Eyring.—1st ed.
p. cm.
ISBN 1-58685-823-8 (first edition)
1. Casserole cookery. 2. One-dish meals. I. Title: One hundred and
one things to do with a casserole. II. Eyring, Janet. III. Title.
TX693.A84 2005
641.8'21—dc22
2005007470

ISBN 978-1-4236-6375-1

To the good people in Hibbard, Idaho, whom we love so dearly. Thank you for accepting us into your community for the year we lived there. And to my dear teachers, especially Mrs. Ruch, Mr. Robertson, and the late Julia Pearson at Clinton Central (Michigan Town, Indiana). Thank you for teaching me to always try my best. —S. A.

To my mother, who had the patience to teach an eight-year-old girl how to cook. —J. E.

CONTENTS

#56–67 Pork

#68–84 Beef

#85–101 Family Favorites

Helpful Hints

- Always grease casserole pans or dishes with nonstick cooking spray for quick cleanup.

- For the best results, use ceramic, glass, or stoneware baking dishes.

- Bake casseroles on the middle oven rack. If possible, avoid the top and bottom racks.

- The first time you try a recipe, check the casserole 5 minutes before its minimum cooking time. Each oven heats differently.

- Many casseroles can be assembled the night before and stored in the refrigerator. Remove casserole from the refrigerator 20 minutes before baking.

- Many casseroles can be assembled and frozen for use at a later date. Move the casserole from the freezer to the refrigerator 24 hours before baking. If casserole was frozen, it may take 10–15 minutes longer to bake. Bake until the temperature at the center of the casserole reaches 160 degrees F.

- Avoid freezing casseroles that contain pasta or rice.

- Low-fat, light, or low-sodium ingredients can be substituted in any recipe.

- When using aluminum foil to cover casseroles, place the shiny side down toward the food. If the shiny side is facing up, it may reflect the heat and possibly increase cooking time.

- Always cook casseroles in a preheated oven.

- Condensed cream of chicken, cream of mushroom, and cream of celery soups can be used interchangeably.

- Precook chicken in large quantities and freeze in 1-cup increments to save preparation time.

BREAKFAST

Asparagus–English Muffin Bake

MAKES 6–8 SERVINGS

1 pound	fresh asparagus, cut into 1-inch pieces
5	English muffins, split and toasted
2 cups	grated Colby Jack cheese, divided
1½ cups	diced fully cooked ham
½ cup	chopped red bell pepper
8	eggs, beaten
2 cups	milk
1 teaspoon	salt
1 teaspoon	dry mustard
½ teaspoon	black pepper

In a 4-quart saucepan, boil asparagus pieces 1 minute. Drain and put in a large bowl of ice water to stop cooking process. Drain and pat asparagus dry with paper towels.

Place English muffin halves, cut side up, to form a crust in a greased 9 x 13-inch pan. Cut the muffins to fill the empty spaces in the pan as needed. Layer asparagus, half the cheese, ham, and bell pepper over muffins.

In a large bowl, whisk eggs, milk, salt, dry mustard, and pepper. Pour the egg mixture evenly over muffins. Cover and refrigerate 2 hours or overnight. Remove from refrigerator before preheating the oven to 375 degrees. Bake 40–45 minutes, or until set in the center. Immediately sprinkle remaining cheese over top and serve.

Blueberry French Toast Casserole

MAKES 6 SERVINGS

1 loaf (20 ounces)	bread, cubed, divided
1 package (8 ounces)	cream cheese, cubed
1 cup	fresh or frozen blueberries
12	eggs, beaten
2 cups	milk
1 teaspoon	vanilla
1/3 cup	maple syrup, plus more for serving
	powdered sugar

Place half the bread cubes in a greased 9 x 13-inch pan. Layer cream cheese cubes evenly over bread. Sprinkle blueberries over top. Cover with the remaining bread cubes.

In a large bowl, whisk eggs, milk, vanilla, and syrup. Drizzle egg mixture evenly over bread. Cover and refrigerate 2 hours or overnight.

Preheat oven to 350 degrees. Cover and bake 30 minutes. Uncover and bake 25–30 minutes more, or until center is firm and top is golden brown. Lightly dust casserole with powdered sugar. Serve with maple syrup.

#3
Baked Breakfast Burritos
MAKES 6–8 SERVINGS

12	eggs
¾ cup	chunky salsa
10	medium flour tortillas
1 can (4 ounces)	chopped green chiles
1 cup	grated cheddar cheese

Preheat oven to 350 degrees.

In a frying pan, scramble eggs and salsa together until firm but not dry. Heat the tortillas in the microwave until softened. Put a spoonful of scrambled egg mixture in the middle of each tortilla. Roll up tortilla and place in a greased 9 x 13-inch pan. Sprinkle with green chiles and cheese. Cover and bake 15 minutes.

Cook and crumble spicy sausage into the scrambled eggs for a heartier breakfast.

Scrambled Egg and Ham Pizza

MAKES 6–8 SERVINGS

1 tube (13.8 ounces)	refrigerated pizza crust dough
8	eggs
2 tablespoons	milk
	salt and pepper, to taste
1½ cups	diced fully cooked ham
1 cup	grated cheddar cheese

Preheat oven to 400 degrees.

Spread pizza crust dough along bottom and halfway up the sides of a greased 9 x 13-inch pan. Bake 8 minutes.

In a frying pan, scramble and cook eggs and milk until firm but not dry. Season with salt and pepper. Spread scrambled eggs over hot crust. Place ham and cheese evenly over eggs. Bake 8–12 minutes, or until crust is golden brown and cheese is melted.

Eggs for Everybody

MAKES 6 SERVINGS

12	eggs
1 cup	milk
1 cup	grated Monterey Jack cheese, divided
1 pound	bacon, cooked and crumbled
1 bunch	green onions, chopped

Preheat oven to 325 degrees.

In a bowl, beat eggs, milk, and half the cheese. Stir in bacon and green onions. Pour mixture into a greased 9 x 13-inch pan. Cover and cook 45–55 minutes, or until eggs are set. Immediately top with remaining cheese and serve.

Sausage and Hash Brown Breakfast Bake

MAKES 6–8 SERVINGS

3 1/2 cups	frozen shredded hash browns
1 pound	sausage, browned and drained
1 cup	grated cheddar cheese
6	eggs, beaten
3/4 cup	milk
1 teaspoon	dry mustard
1/2 teaspoon	salt
1/2 teaspoon	black pepper

Spread hash browns into bottom of a greased 9 x 13-inch pan. Sprinkle cooked sausage and cheese over top.

In a bowl, combine eggs, milk, dry mustard, salt, and pepper. Pour egg mixture evenly over sausage and hash browns. Cover and refrigerate 2 hours or overnight.

Remove from refrigerator 20 minutes before baking and preheat oven to 350 degrees. Cover and bake 30 minutes. Uncover and bake 5–8 minutes more, or until center is set.

Southwestern Eggs

MAKES 6 SERVINGS

12	eggs
½ cup	milk
2 cans (4 ounces each)	chopped green chiles
½ cup	chopped red bell pepper
1 cup	grated cheddar cheese
1 cup	grated Monterey Jack cheese

Preheat oven to 350 degrees.

In a bowl, beat eggs and milk. Set aside.

In a greased 9 x 13-inch pan, layer chiles, bell pepper, and cheese. Pour egg mixture over top. Cover and bake 30–40 minutes, or until eggs are set in the center.

Omelet Brunch

MAKES 6–8 SERVINGS

18	**eggs**
1 cup	**sour cream**
1 cup	**milk**
1 teaspoon	**salt**
¼ cup	**chopped green onions**
1 cup	**grated cheddar cheese**

Preheat oven to 325 degrees.

In a large bowl, beat eggs, sour cream, milk, and salt. Fold in green onions. Pour mixture into a greased 9 x 13-inch pan. Bake 45–55 minutes, or until eggs are set. Immediately sprinkle cheese over top and cut into squares before serving.

Crescent, Hash Brown, and Sausage Bake

MAKES 4–6 SERVINGS

1 tube (8 ounces)	refrigerated crescent roll dough
1 package (10.4 ounces)	sausage links, browned, drained, and sliced
1 cup	frozen shredded hash browns
1½ cups	grated cheddar cheese
5	eggs
⅓ cup	milk
	salt and pepper, to taste
	salsa, for serving

Preheat oven to 375 degrees.

Unroll crescents and press dough over bottom and up the sides of a 12-inch round pizza pan. (Dough up the sides of the pan should have a small lip so when the egg mixture is added, it stays in the crust.) Sprinkle sausage, hash browns, and cheese over dough.

In a bowl, beat eggs, milk, salt, and pepper with a fork. Pour egg mixture over dough. Bake 30 minutes. Serve wedges with fresh salsa.

Raisin French Toast Casserole

MAKES 6 SERVINGS

1 loaf (24 ounces)	**cinnamon raisin bread, cubed**
6	**eggs, slightly beaten**
3 cups	**milk**
2 teaspoons	**vanilla**
	powdered sugar
	maple syrup, for serving

Place bread cubes into a greased 9 x 13-inch pan.

In a bowl, whisk eggs, milk, and vanilla. Pour egg mixture evenly over bread. Cover and refrigerate 2 hours or overnight.

Remove from refrigerator 20 minutes before baking and preheat oven to 350 degrees. Bake, uncovered, 45–50 minutes, or until golden brown. Sprinkle powdered sugar over top. Serve with maple syrup.

Spinach Frittata

MAKES 2–4 SERVINGS

4	**eggs**
1½ cups	**milk**
½ teaspoon	**salt**
1 package (10 ounces)	**frozen spinach, thawed and drained**
¾ cup	**grated cheddar or Swiss cheese**

Preheat oven to 400 degrees.

In a bowl, beat eggs, milk, and salt together. Pour mixture into a greased 8 x 8-inch pan. Spread spinach over egg mixture. Bake 17–22 minutes, or until eggs have set. Sprinkle cheese over top.

Large eggs work best for this recipe.

Swiss and Sausage Casserole

MAKES 6–8 SERVINGS

10	slices white bread, cubed
1 pound	spicy sausage, browned and drained
1 can (4 ounces)	sliced mushrooms, drained
$3/4$ cup	grated cheddar cheese
$1\frac{1}{2}$ cups	grated Swiss cheese
8	eggs, beaten
2 cups	half-and-half
2 cups	milk
1 teaspoon	salt
1 teaspoon	black pepper

Place bread cubes in a greased 9 x 13-inch pan. Crumble cooked sausage over bread. Evenly lay mushrooms over sausage and sprinkle cheeses over top.

In a large bowl, mix eggs, half-and-half, milk, salt, and pepper. Pour egg mixture evenly over cheese. Cover and refrigerate 2 hours or overnight.

Remove from refrigerator 20 minutes before baking and preheat oven to 350 degrees. Cover and bake 30 minutes. Uncover and bake 15–20 minutes more.

VEGETABLE

Asparagus Casserole

MAKES 4 SERVINGS

1 cup	grated cheddar cheese
2 cups	crushed saltine crackers
¼ cup	butter or margarine, melted
1 can (10.75 ounces)	condensed cream of mushroom soup
1 can (15 ounces)	asparagus spears, drained with liquid reserved
½ cup	sliced almonds

Preheat oven to 350 degrees.

In a bowl, combine cheese and cracker crumbs. Set aside.

In a separate bowl, mix together butter, soup, and the liquid from the can of asparagus.

Layer half the cracker mixture into bottom of an 8 x 8-inch pan. Arrange half the asparagus spears over top. Layer half the sliced almonds and half the soup mixture over asparagus. Layer remaining asparagus spears, almonds, and soup mixture over top. Cover with remaining cracker mixture.

Bake 20–25 minutes, or until bubbly and golden brown.

Stacked Black Bean Tortilla Pie

MAKES 4–5 SERVINGS

1 can (16 ounces)	refried beans
1 cup	salsa, divided, plus more for serving
1 teaspoon	minced garlic
1 tablespoon	dried cilantro
1 can (15 ounces)	black beans, rinsed and drained
1	medium tomato, chopped
7	medium flour tortillas
2 cups	grated cheddar cheese
	sour cream, for serving

Preheat oven to 400 degrees.

In a bowl, combine refried beans, $3/4$ cup salsa, and garlic.

In a separate bowl, combine remaining salsa, cilantro, black beans, and tomato.

Place a tortilla in the bottom of a greased pie pan. Spread a fourth of the refried bean mixture over tortilla within $1/2$ inch of edge. Sprinkle $1/4$ cup cheese over beans and cover with another tortilla. Spoon a third of the black bean mixture over tortilla. Sprinkle $1/4$ cup cheese over black bean mixture and cover with another tortilla. Repeat layers, ending with a final layer of refried bean mixture spread over last tortilla. Sprinkle with $1/2$ cup cheese.

Cover and bake 35–40 minutes. Serve with salsa and sour cream.

Chunky Veggie Casserole

MAKES 6–8 SERVINGS

2 cups	water
1 cup	uncooked white rice
1 bag (16 ounces)	frozen broccoli florets
1 bag (16 ounces)	frozen cauliflower florets
1/3 cup	water
1	medium onion, chopped
1/3 cup	butter or margarine
1 jar (16 ounces)	cheddar cheese dip
1 can (10.75 ounces)	condensed cream of chicken soup
2/3 cup	milk

In a saucepan, bring 2 cups water and rice to a boil. Reduce heat. Cover and simmer 15 minutes, or until water is absorbed.

In a bowl, heat broccoli and cauliflower with 1/3 cup water in microwave on high heat 8 minutes, or until done. Drain vegetables.

Preheat oven to 350 degrees.

In a frying pan, sauté onion in butter. Stir cooked rice into onion. Spread rice mixture into a greased 9 x 13-inch pan. Stir vegetables, cheese sauce, soup, and milk into rice mixture. Bake 30–35 minutes, or until bubbly.

Mozzarella Potatoes

MAKES 4 SERVINGS

4	medium potatoes, peeled
4	Roma tomatoes, sliced
1	large green bell pepper, seeded and cut into strips
	salt and pepper, to taste
1 teaspoon	Italian seasoning
2 cups	grated mozzarella cheese
1 cup	sour cream

Preheat oven to 400 degrees.

In a stockpot, boil potatoes 25–30 minutes until partially cooked, then thinly slice.

Layer half each of the potato slices, tomato slices, and bell pepper strips in a greased 9 x 9-inch pan. Season with salt and pepper.

Sprinkle half each of the Italian seasoning and mozzarella cheese over vegetables. Repeat layers with remaining potatoes, tomatoes, and bell pepper. Sprinkle remaining seasoning and cheese over vegetables, then spread sour cream over top. Cover and bake 30–40 minutes, or until bubbly.

Creamy Spinach Casserole

MAKES 4–6 SERVINGS

2 packages (10 ounces each)	**frozen chopped spinach**
1 envelope	**onion soup mix**
1 container (16 ounces)	**sour cream**
³⁄₄ cup	**grated cheddar cheese**

Preheat oven to 350 degrees.

Cook spinach according to package directions and drain. Place in a greased 1½- to 2-quart baking dish. Stir in onion soup mix and sour cream. Sprinkle cheese over top. Bake 20–25 minutes, or until bubbly.

Grandma's Yummy Potatoes

MAKES 6–8 SERVINGS

8	medium potatoes
1 cup	grated cheddar cheese
¼ cup	butter or margarine, melted
1 can (10.75 ounces)	condensed cream of chicken soup
½ cup	chopped onion
1 small jar	diced pimientos
1 container (16 ounces)	sour cream
¾ cup	crushed corn flakes or potato chips

Preheat oven to 350 degrees.

Peel and shred potatoes. Boil shredded potatoes in water 10–15 minutes and drain.

Stir cheese, butter, soup, onion, pimientos, and sour cream into potatoes. Spread potato mixture into a greased 9 x 13-inch pan. Bake, uncovered, 45–55 minutes, or until bubbly. Sprinkle corn flakes over potatoes and bake 5 minutes more.

For a more traditional potato dish, eliminate the pimientos.

Green Bean Casserole

MAKES 4–6 SERVINGS

2 cans (14.5 ounces each)	**French-cut green beans, drained**
1 can (10.75 ounces)	**condensed cream of mushroom soup**
$\frac{2}{3}$ cup	**milk**
$\frac{1}{3}$ cup	**real bacon bits**
$\frac{1}{4}$ teaspoon	**black pepper**
$1\frac{1}{4}$ cups	**French-fried onions, divided**

Preheat oven to 350 degrees.

Combine green beans, soup, milk, bacon bits, and black pepper in a greased $1\frac{1}{2}$- to 2-quart baking dish. Stir in $\frac{1}{2}$ cup onions. Bake, uncovered, 30 minutes, or until bubbly. Sprinkle remaining onions over top and bake 5 minutes more.

5–7 slices of bacon, cooked and crumbled, may be substituted.

Hominy Casserole

MAKES 4–5 SERVINGS

1	medium onion, chopped
1	large green bell pepper, seeded and diced
$\frac{1}{2}$ cup	butter or margarine
1 can (15.5 ounces)	white hominy, drained
1 can (15.5 ounces)	yellow hominy, drained
1 can (12 ounces)	whole-kernel corn, drained
1 can (4 ounces)	sliced mushrooms, drained
$\frac{1}{4}$ cup	grated Parmesan cheese
1 cup	cheddar cheese dip, such as Cheez Whiz
$\frac{1}{4}$ cup	diced pimiento, drained

Preheat oven to 350 degrees.

In a frying pan, sauté onion and bell pepper in butter until tender. Stir white and yellow hominy, corn, mushrooms, Parmesan, cheese dip, and pimento into onion mixture. Spread into a greased 8 x 8-inch pan. Bake 30–35 minutes, or until bubbly.

Indiana Corn Lover's Casserole

MAKES 4–6 SERVINGS

2	eggs, slightly beaten
1 can (14.75 ounces)	cream-style corn
1 can (12 ounces)	whole-kernel corn, drained
³⁄₄ cup	sour cream
3 tablespoons	butter or margarine, melted
1½ cups	grated cheddar cheese
1	medium onion, chopped
1 can (4 ounces)	chopped green chiles, drained
1 package (6.5 ounces)	corn muffin mix

Preheat oven to 350 degrees.

In a large bowl, combine eggs, corn, sour cream, butter, cheese, onion, and chiles. Gently fold in corn muffin mix until moistened. Spread mixture into a greased 2-quart baking dish. Bake 60–70 minutes, or until golden brown on top and center is set.

Rice and Green Chile Casserole

MAKES 4–6 SERVINGS

1 box (6 ounces)	instant long grain and wild rice mix
1 cup	sour cream
1 can (4 ounces)	chopped green chiles, drained
1 cup	grated cheddar cheese
1 cup	grated Monterey Jack cheese

Prepare rice according to package directions.

Preheat oven to 350 degrees.

In a bowl, mix together sour cream and green chiles. Spread half the cooked rice over bottom of a greased 8 x 8-inch pan. Spoon half the sour cream mixture over rice. Sprinkle half of each cheese over top. Spoon remaining rice over cheese. Spread remaining sour cream mixture over rice, then sprinkle remaining cheese over top. Bake, uncovered, 15–20 minutes, or until bubbly.

Mexican-Inspired Pizza

MAKES 5–7 SERVINGS

1 tube (13.8 ounces)	**refrigerated pizza crust dough**
1 can (16 ounces)	**refried beans**
3/4 cup	**chunky salsa**
1 envelope	**taco seasoning**
1 1/2 cups	**grated Mexican-blend cheese**
1 bag (10 ounces)	**shredded lettuce**
2	**Roma tomatoes, diced**
1 1/2 cups	**crushed nacho cheese tortilla chips**

Preheat oven to 400 degrees.

Cover bottom and partially up the sides of a greased 9 x 13-inch pan with pizza dough. Bake 10–12 minutes, or until light golden brown.

In a saucepan, heat refried beans and salsa together until bubbly. Stir taco seasoning into refried bean mixture. Spread refried bean mixture over baked crust. Sprinkle cheese over beans and bake 5–8 minutes, or until cheese is melted. Layer lettuce, tomatoes, and crushed tortilla chips over top and serve immediately.

Sweet Onion Casserole

MAKES 6 SERVINGS

6	large sweet onions, thinly sliced
6 tablespoons	butter or margarine, divided
1 can (10.75 ounces)	condensed cream of celery soup
1/3 cup	milk
1/2 teaspoon	black pepper
2 cups	grated Swiss cheese, divided
6	slices French bread, cut 1-inch thick

In a large frying pan, sauté onions in 4 tablespoons butter 11–13 minutes, or until onions are tender.

In a large bowl, combine soup, milk, pepper, and 1 1/2 cups cheese.

Preheat oven to 350 degrees. Stir onions into soup mixture. Spread mixture into a greased 9 x 13-inch pan. Sprinkle remaining cheese over top. Melt remaining butter and brush it over one side of each bread slice. Place bread slices, butter side up, in the pan, making three rows. Bake 24–28 minutes. Cool 5–7 minutes before serving.

Other varieties of condensed cream soups may be substituted.

Veggie Shepherd's Pie

MAKES 4 SERVINGS

1 bag (16 ounces)	**frozen California-blend vegetables**
1 can (10.75 ounces)	**condensed cheddar cheese soup**
½ teaspoon	**thyme**
2 cups	**mashed potatoes, seasoned with garlic**

Preheat oven to 350 degrees.

In a greased 9 x 9-inch pan, combine frozen vegetables, soup, and thyme. Spread potatoes evenly over vegetable layer. Cover and bake 25 minutes. Uncover and bake 15–20 minutes more, or until heated through.

Instant potatoes may be substituted.

Vegetable Stuffing Casserole

MAKES 7–9 SERVINGS

1 bag (16 ounces)	frozen green beans
1 bag (16 ounces)	frozen mixed vegetables
2 cans (10.75 ounces each)	condensed cream of mushroom soup
1 can (6 ounces)	French-fried onions
1 box (6 ounces)	seasoned stuffing mix
3 tablespoons	butter or margarine, melted
$1/4$ cup	water

Preheat oven to 350 degrees.

Pour frozen vegetables into bottom of a greased 9 x 13-inch pan. Stir soup into vegetables. Sprinkle onions and stuffing mix evenly over top. Drizzle melted butter and water over stuffing layer. Cover and bake 55–65 minutes, or until heated through.

Baked Cheesy Zucchini

MAKES 4 SERVINGS

1 medium	zucchini, thinly sliced
1	sweet onion, thinly sliced
2	Roma tomatoes, thinly sliced
2 tablespoons	butter or margarine, melted
3/4 cup	Italian-flavored breadcrumbs
1 cup	grated mozzarella cheese

Preheat oven to 350 degrees.

In a greased 9 x 9-inch pan, layer zucchini, onion, and tomatoes. Drizzle butter over vegetables. Sprinkle breadcrumbs over top. Cover and bake 45–50 minutes, or until vegetables are tender. Remove from oven, uncover, and sprinkle cheese over top. Bake 5–7 minutes more, or until cheese is bubbly.

CHICKEN

Broccoli and Chicken Casserole

MAKES 4–6 SERVINGS

2 cups	chopped cooked chicken
1 can (10.75 ounces)	condensed cream of mushroom soup
1/4 cup	milk
3/4 cup	grated Monterey Jack cheese
1 package (10 ounces)	frozen broccoli, thawed
1/2 cup	green onion, sliced
1/2 teaspoon	black pepper

Preheat oven to 350 degrees.

In a large bowl, mix chicken, soup, milk, cheese, broccoli, green onion, and black pepper together. Spread mixture into a greased 9 x 13-inch pan. Bake 35–40 minutes, or until bubbly.

Cashew Chicken

MAKES 2–4 SERVINGS

1 package (6.2 ounces)	**fried rice, with seasoning packet**
2 cups	**water**
2	**boneless, skinless chicken breasts, cooked and cubed**
½ cup	**sliced celery**
1 can (4 ounces)	**water chestnuts, drained**
⅔ cup	**cashews**

Preheat oven to 350 degrees.

In a bowl, combine rice, seasoning packet, and water.

Layer chicken, rice mixture, celery, and water chestnuts in a greased 9 x 9-inch pan. Cover and bake 30–40 minutes, or until rice is done. Sprinkle with cashews.

Cheesy Chicken
MAKES 4–6 SERVINGS

4 to 6	boneless, skinless chicken breasts
1 container (16 ounces)	sour cream
1 can (10.75 ounces)	condensed cream of celery soup
1 can (10.75 ounces)	condensed cream of chicken soup
1¼ cups	water
2 cups	uncooked white rice
1 cup	grated cheddar cheese

Preheat oven to 325 degrees.

Place chicken in a greased 9 x 13-inch pan.

In a bowl, combine sour cream, soups, water, and uncooked rice. Pour over chicken. Cover and bake 1 hour. Sprinkle with cheese immediately before serving.

Ritzy Chicken

MAKES 4 SERVINGS

4	boneless, skinless chicken breasts
1 can (10.75 ounces)	condensed cream of chicken soup
1 can (10.75 ounces)	condensed cheddar broccoli soup
1/3 cup	milk
1 1/2 cups	sour cream
2 cups	cooked white rice
25 to 35	butter-flavor crackers, crumbled

Preheat oven to 375 degrees.

Place chicken in a greased 9 x 13-inch pan.

In a bowl, combine soups, milk, sour cream, and rice. Pour over chicken. Bake 45 minutes, or until chicken is done. During last 5–10 minutes of baking, sprinkle cracker crumbs over top.

Tortilla Chip Enchiladas

MAKES 6–8 SERVINGS

2 cups	chopped cooked chicken
2 cans (10.75 ounces each)	condensed cream of chicken soup
1 cup	sour cream
¼ cup	chopped onion
1 bag (12 ounces)	tortilla chips, crushed in bag
1 cup	grated Monterey Jack cheese
½ cup	salsa, for serving

Preheat oven to 350 degrees.

In a large bowl combine chicken, soup, sour cream, and onion.

In a greased 9 x 13-inch pan, layer half the chips and half the soup mixture. Repeat layers. Top with cheese and bake 30 minutes. Serve with salsa.

Cornbread-Chicken Casserole

MAKES 6 SERVINGS

4 cups	**uncooked egg noodles**
3 cups	**chopped cooked chicken**
2 cans (10.75 ounces each)	**condensed cream of celery soup**
1 can (15 ounces)	**cream-style corn**
2 cups	**grated cheddar cheese**
1 package	**cornbread mix (8 x 8-inch pan size)**

Preheat oven to 350 degrees.

Boil noodles 5–7 minutes, or until cooked. Drain and mix with chicken, soup, corn, and cheese. Pour noodle mixture into a greased 9 x 13-inch pan.

In a bowl, combine cornbread mix with ingredients listed on package. Spoon cornbread batter over noodle mixture. Bake 25–30 minutes, or until cornbread top is golden brown.

Family-Friendly Chicken Enchiladas

MAKES 6–8 SERVINGS

3 cups	cooked and shredded chicken
2 cans (10.75 ounces each)	condensed cream of chicken soup
1 cup	sour cream
1 can (4 ounces)	diced green chiles, drained
¼ cup	dried minced onion
2½ cups	grated cheddar cheese, divided
10	medium flour tortillas
⅓ cup	milk

Preheat oven to 350 degrees.

In a large bowl, combine chicken, 1 can soup, sour cream, chiles, onion, and 1½ cups cheese. Fill each tortilla with ⅓ to ½ cup chicken mixture. Roll filled tortillas and place seam side down in a greased 9 x 13-inch pan. Combine remaining soup with milk and spread over tortilla rolls. Sprinkle remaining cheese over top. Cover and bake 25 minutes. Uncover and bake 5–10 minutes more, or until heated through.

1 can (10 ounces) enchilada sauce can be used to top enchiladas in place of the soup-and-milk mixture.

Fiesta Chicken Casserole

MAKES 4–6 SERVINGS

2 cups	uncooked small shell pasta
2 cups	chopped cooked chicken
1 jar (16 ounces)	medium salsa
2 cups	grated Mexican-blend cheese

Preheat oven to 350 degrees.

Cook pasta according to package directions and drain. Combine noodles, chicken, salsa, and cheese in a greased 9 x 13-inch pan. Cover and bake 20–25 minutes, or until heated through.

Mango Chicken

MAKES 4 SERVINGS

1 cup	uncooked white rice
2 cups	water
4	boneless, skinless chicken breasts
1 jar (12 ounces)	mango salsa

Preheat oven to 350 degrees.

In a greased 9 x 13-inch pan, combine rice and water. Lay chicken over rice and pour mango salsa over top. Cover and bake 1 hour.

#37

Creamy Chicken and Rice

MAKES 4–6 SERVINGS

2 cups	**uncooked white rice**
2 cans (10.75 ounces each)	**condensed cream of chicken soup**
2 cups	**water**
1 envelope	**onion soup mix, divided**
4 to 6	**boneless, skinless chicken breasts**

Preheat oven to 375 degrees.

In a bowl, combine rice, chicken soup, water, and half the onion soup mix. Spread mixture into a greased 9 x 13-inch pan. Lay chicken over top. Sprinkle remaining onion soup mix over chicken. Cover and bake 2 hours.

This casserole can also be baked at 300 degrees for 3 hours.

Grandma's Chicken Potpie

MAKES 5–7 SERVINGS

2 cups	frozen Normandy or California-style vegetables
1½ cups	cubed cooked chicken
2 cans (10.75 ounces each)	condensed cream of chicken soup
¾ cup	milk
½ teaspoon	thyme or rosemary
½ teaspoon	black pepper
1 can (10 ounces)	refrigerated flaky biscuits

Preheat oven to 400 degrees.

Cook and cut vegetables into bite-size pieces.

In a greased 3-quart baking dish, combine all vegetables, chicken, soup, milk, and seasonings. Bake, uncovered, 15 minutes, then remove from oven and stir.

Quickly cut biscuits in half. Place biscuit halves, cut side down, over hot chicken and vegetable mixture. Bake 15–20 minutes more, or until biscuits are golden brown and done in the center.

Green Bean and Chicken Casserole

MAKES 4 SERVINGS

1 tablespoon	olive oil
4	boneless, skinless chicken breasts
3 to 4 cans (14.5 ounces each)	French-cut green beans, drained
1 can (10.75 ounces)	condensed cream of mushroom or chicken soup
3/4 cup	mayonnaise
1 teaspoon	garlic powder
1/3 cup	grated Parmesan cheese

Preheat oven to 350 degrees.

In a large frying pan, heat olive oil. Lightly brown chicken 3 minutes on each side. Meanwhile, spread green beans evenly in bottom of a greased 9 x 13-inch pan. Lay chicken over green beans.

In a bowl, combine soup, mayonnaise, and garlic powder. Spread soup mixture evenly over chicken and beans. Sprinkle Parmesan over top. Bake, uncovered, 35–40 minutes, or until chicken is done.

Home-Style Chicken Casserole

MAKES 6 SERVINGS

4 cups	**frozen shredded hash browns, thawed**
1 can (6 ounces)	**French-fried onions, divided**
6 slices	**processed American cheese**
2	**boneless, skinless chicken breasts, cubed**
1 can (10.75 ounces)	**condensed cream of chicken soup**
³⁄₄ cup	**milk**
1 can (12 ounces)	**whole-kernel corn, drained**

Preheat oven to 375 degrees.

In a large bowl, stir hash browns and half the onions together. Spread mixture into a greased 9 x 13-inch pan. Lay cheese slices evenly over hash browns. Place chicken cubes evenly over top.

In the bowl, stir together soup and milk. Pour soup mixture over chicken. Bake, uncovered, 30 minutes. Spoon corn over chicken, and then stir in the pan. Bake, uncovered, 15 minutes more. Sprinkle remaining onions over top. Bake an additional 5 minutes. Let cool 5–7 minutes before serving.

Sweet Lemony Chicken

MAKES 6 SERVINGS

6	boneless, skinless chicken breasts
2 tablespoons	butter or margarine, melted
1/3 cup	flour
1/3 cup	honey
1/4 cup	lemon juice
1 tablespoon	soy sauce

Preheat oven to 350 degrees.

Place the butter in one medium bowl and the flour in another. Dip chicken in butter and then in flour. Place in a greased 9 x 13-inch pan. In a small bowl, combine honey, lemon juice, and soy sauce. Pour sauce over chicken. Cover and bake 40 minutes, or until chicken is done.

Pineapple Chicken

MAKES 6–8 SERVINGS

2 cups	diced cooked chicken
1 can (8 ounces)	crushed pineapple, with liquid
1 cup	chopped celery
1 cup	cooked white rice
1 can (10.75 ounces)	condensed cream of mushroom soup
1 cup	mayonnaise
1 can (6 ounces)	sliced water chestnuts, drained
2 cups	breadcrumbs
1 tablespoon	butter or margarine, melted

Preheat oven to 350 degrees.

In a large bowl, combine chicken, pineapple, celery, rice, soup, mayonnaise, and water chestnuts. Transfer mixture to a greased 9 x 13-inch pan. In the bowl, combine breadcrumbs and butter; sprinkle over top of chicken mixture. Bake 30–45 minutes.

Southwestern Chicken Roll-ups

MAKES 4–6 SERVINGS

1 cup	finely crushed cheese crackers
1 envelope	taco seasoning
4 to 6	boneless, skinless chicken breasts
4 to 6	slices Monterey Jack cheese
1 can (4 ounces)	chopped green chiles

Preheat oven to 350 degrees.

On a plate, combine crackers and taco seasoning.

Flatten chicken with a meat tenderizer and place 1 slice cheese and about 1 tablespoon chiles on each piece of chicken. Roll chicken and secure with a toothpick.

Sprinkle chicken with cracker mixture and place in a greased 9 x 13-inch pan. Bake, uncovered, 35–40 minutes, or until chicken is done. Remember to remove toothpicks before serving.

Swiss Chicken

MAKES 4–6 SERVINGS

4 to 6	**boneless, skinless chicken breasts**
4 to 6	**slices Swiss cheese**
1 can (10.75 ounces)	**condensed cream of mushroom soup**
¼ cup	**milk**
1 box (6 ounces)	**seasoned stuffing mix**
¼ cup	**butter or margarine, melted**

Preheat oven to 350 degrees.

Lay chicken in bottom of a greased 9 x 13-inch pan. Place cheese slices over chicken.

In a bowl, mix together soup and milk. Spoon soup mixture over chicken. Sprinkle dry stuffing mix over soup layer and drizzle butter over top. Cover and bake 55–65 minutes, or until chicken is done.

Cream of chicken soup may be substituted for cream of mushroom.

Teriyaki Chicken

MAKES 4 SERVINGS

2	boneless, skinless chicken breasts, cubed
1 can (15 ounces)	chicken broth
2 tablespoons	brown sugar
2 tablespoons	soy sauce
½ teaspoon	ground ginger
½ teaspoon	Worcestershire sauce
1 cup	uncooked white rice
1 can (8 ounces)	pineapple chunks, drained

Preheat oven to 350 degrees.

Combine chicken, broth, brown sugar, soy sauce, ginger, Worcestershire sauce, rice, and pineapple in a large bowl. Transfer mixture to a greased 9 x 13-inch pan. Cover and bake 1 hour, or until rice is done.

Wild Rice and Chicken

MAKES 4 SERVINGS

1 package (6.2 ounces)	**long grain and wild rice, with seasoning packet**
1½ cups	**water**
4	**boneless, skinless chicken breasts**
½ teaspoon	**basil**
½ teaspoon	**garlic powder**

Preheat oven to 375 degrees.

In a bowl, combine rice, seasoning packet, and water. Pour mixture into a greased 9 x 13-inch pan. Place chicken over rice mixture and sprinkle with basil and garlic powder. Cover and bake 1 hour.

Delicious Chicken

MAKES 4–6 SERVINGS

3 tablespoons	butter or margarine, melted
3 cups	peeled and thinly sliced potatoes
1 package (16 ounces)	frozen corn
2 teaspoons	salt, divided
2 teaspoons	basil, divided
1 cup	graham cracker crumbs
1/3 cup	butter or margarine, melted
4 to 6	boneless, skinless chicken breasts

Preheat oven to 375 degrees.

Pour 3 tablespoons melted butter in the bottom of a 9 x 13-inch pan. Combine potatoes and corn in the pan, and then sprinkle with 1 teaspoon salt and 1 teaspoon basil.

In a small bowl, combine cracker crumbs and remaining salt and basil. Transfer mixture to a plate.

Dip chicken in 1/3 cup melted butter then roll in crumb mixture, coating completely. Place chicken over vegetables. Cover and bake 60–75 minutes, or until chicken is done and vegetables are tender. Remove from oven, uncover, and bake 10 minutes more to brown chicken.

TURKEY

After-Thanksgiving Casserole

MAKES 4–6 SERVINGS

1 box (6 ounces)	seasoned stuffing mix
3 cups	chopped cooked turkey
2 cups	turkey gravy, divided
2 cups	mashed potatoes, seasoned with garlic

Preheat oven to 350 degrees.

Prepare stuffing according to package directions. Spoon stuffing into a greased 2-quart baking dish. Lay turkey over stuffing. Pour 1 cup gravy over turkey. Spread mashed potatoes evenly over top. Cover with remaining gravy. Cover and bake 35–45 minutes, or until bubbly.

Try adding $3/4$ cup frozen peas as a layer between the stuffing and the turkey.

Turkey Tortilla Casserole

MAKES 6–8 SERVINGS

3 cups	chopped cooked turkey
1 can (4 ounces)	chopped green chiles
¾ cup	chicken broth
2 cans (10.75 ounces each)	condensed cream of chicken soup
1	medium onion, chopped
8 to 10	medium gordita-style flour tortillas
2 cups	grated Monterey Jack cheese

Preheat oven to 350 degrees.

In a large bowl, combine turkey, chiles, broth, soup, and onion. Cover bottom of a greased 9 x 13-inch pan with half the tortillas. Spread half the turkey mixture over tortilla layer. Sprinkle half the cheese over top. Repeat layers. Bake 25–30 minutes, or until bubbly and heated through.

Paula's Turketti

MAKES 6–8 SERVINGS

1 can (10.75 ounces)	**condensed cream of mushroom soup**
½ cup	**water**
2 cups	**cubed cooked turkey**
1⅓ cups	**broken spaghetti, cooked and drained**
⅓ cup	**chopped green bell pepper**
½ cup	**chopped onion**
½ teaspoon	**salt**
¼ teaspoon	**black pepper**
2 cups	**grated cheddar cheese, divided**

Preheat oven to 350 degrees.

In a large bowl, combine soup and water. Stir in turkey, spaghetti, bell pepper, onion, salt, pepper, and 1 cup cheese. Spread mixture in a greased 9 x 13-inch pan. Sprinkle remaining 1 cup cheese over top. Bake 45 minutes.

Poppy Seed Casserole

MAKES 6 SERVINGS

1½ pounds	ground turkey
1	green or red bell pepper, chopped
3 cans (8 ounces each)	tomato sauce
½ teaspoon	salt
½ teaspoon	black pepper
1 package (8 ounces)	cream cheese, cubed
½ cup	sour cream
1 cup	cottage cheese
1 tablespoon	poppy seeds
1 bag (12–18 ounces)	curly noodles, cooked and drained
1 teaspoon	Italian seasoning
½ cup	grated Parmesan cheese

Preheat oven to 350 degrees.

Brown turkey and bell pepper together until turkey is done. Drain off liquid. Add tomato sauce, salt, and pepper and simmer over low heat.

In a bowl, combine cream cheese, sour cream, cottage cheese, and poppy seeds, and mix with noodles. Add noodle mixture to a greased 9 x 13-inch pan. Top with turkey mixture. Cover and bake 30 minutes. Uncover and bake 10 minutes more. Sprinkle Italian seasoning and Parmesan over top.

For a more saucy dish, add an extra can of tomato sauce.

Stuffing and Turkey Casserole

MAKES 6 SERVINGS

2 cans (10.75 ounces each)	**condensed cream of celery soup**
1 cup	**milk**
½ teaspoon	**black pepper**
1 bag (16 ounces)	**frozen mixed vegetables, thawed and drained**
2½ cups	**cubed cooked turkey**
1 box (6 ounces)	**seasoned stuffing mix**

Preheat oven to 400 degrees.

Mix together soup, milk, pepper, vegetables, and turkey. Spread turkey mixture into a greased 9 x 13-inch pan. Prepare stuffing according to package directions. Spoon stuffing evenly over turkey. Bake 25 minutes, or until heated through.

For a thicker layer of stuffing, use 2 boxes of stuffing.

Turkey and Potato Bake

MAKES 4 SERVINGS

2 cups	**cubed cooked turkey**
2	**medium potatoes, peeled and thinly sliced**
1	**medium onion, sliced**
	salt and pepper, to taste
1 can (10.75 ounces)	**condensed cream of celery soup**
½ cup	**skim milk**

Preheat oven to 350 degrees.

In a greased 8 x 8-inch pan, layer turkey, potatoes, and onion. Sprinkle with salt and pepper.

In a bowl, combine soup and milk. Pour over turkey. Cover and bake 1 hour.

Easy Turkey Divan

MAKES 4–6 SERVINGS

2 cups	diced cooked turkey
1 package (10 ounces)	frozen broccoli spears, cooked
1 can (10.75 ounces)	condensed cream of chicken soup
1/2 cup	mayonnaise
1/2 teaspoon	lemon juice
1/4 teaspoon	curry powder
1/2 cup	grated sharp cheddar cheese

Preheat oven to 350 degrees.

Layer turkey and broccoli in a greased 9 x 13-inch pan.

In a bowl, combine soup, mayonnaise, lemon juice, and curry powder. Pour over turkey and sprinkle with cheese. Cover and bake 40 minutes.

Turkey Noodle Casserole

MAKES 4–6 SERVINGS

1 bag (12 ounces)	**egg noodles**
1 can (10.75 ounces)	**condensed cream of celery soup**
½ cup	**milk**
1 can (5 ounces)	**turkey, drained**
2 cups	**grated cheddar cheese**
½ cup	**crushed potato chips**

Preheat oven to 400 degrees.

Cook noodles according to package directions and drain. Stir soup, milk, turkey, and cheese into hot noodles. Spread noodle mixture into a greased 2-quart baking dish. Bake 15 minutes. Top with crushed potato chips and bake 3–5 minutes more.

PORK

Baked Ravioli Alfredo

MAKES 6 SERVINGS

1 bag (25 ounces)	frozen Italian-sausage ravioli
1 bag (16 ounces)	frozen broccoli florets
1 jar (16 ounces)	Alfredo sauce
$3/4$ cup	milk
$1/4$ cup	seasoned breadcrumbs

Preheat oven to 350 degrees.

Place frozen ravioli into bottom of a greased 9 x 13-inch pan. Spread broccoli over ravioli. Pour Alfredo sauce over broccoli. Drizzle milk evenly over top. Cover and bake 50 minutes. Uncover and sprinkle breadcrumbs over top. Bake, uncovered, 10 minutes more, or until heated through.

Sausage and Spaghetti Casserole

MAKES 6–8 SERVINGS

1 pound	sausage
1	medium onion, chopped
1 jar (26 ounces)	spaghetti sauce
½ cup	water
1 package (16 ounces)	spaghetti noodles, cooked and drained
¼ cup	butter or margarine, melted
3	eggs, beaten
½ cup	grated Parmesan cheese
2 cups	grated mozzarella cheese, divided
1 container (16 ounces)	cottage cheese

Preheat oven to 350 degrees.

In a frying pan, brown sausage and onion together and drain any excess grease. Stir spaghetti sauce and water into sausage mixture. Allow sauce to simmer over low heat 5 minutes.

In a bowl, combine cooked spaghetti, butter, eggs, Parmesan, and half the mozzarella cheese. Spread noodle mixture into a greased 9 x 13-inch pan. Evenly spread cottage cheese over noodles. Spread spaghetti sauce mixture evenly over top. Sprinkle remaining cheese over sauce. Cover and bake 25 minutes. Uncover and bake 10–15 minutes more.

Canadian Bacon Pizza Bake

MAKES 6 SERVINGS

2 tubes (7.5 ounces each)	**refrigerated buttermilk biscuits**
1 jar (14 ounces)	**pizza sauce**
1 cup	**grated Italian-blend cheese**
15 to 20 slices	**Canadian bacon**
1½ cups	**grated mozzarella cheese, divided**

Preheat oven to 375 degrees.

Separate biscuits and cut each one into 4 pieces. Place in a large bowl and toss with pizza sauce and Italian-blend cheese. Place biscuit mixture into a greased 9 x 13-inch pan. Place Canadian bacon slices evenly over top. Sprinkle mozzarella cheese over top. Bake 20–25 minutes, or until biscuits are done.

Broccoli and Ham Potpie

MAKES 4–6 SERVINGS

1 package (10 ounces)	frozen chopped broccoli, thawed
1 can (15 ounces)	whole-kernel corn, drained
1 can (10.75 ounces)	condensed cream of mushroom soup
2 cups	chopped fully cooked ham
1$^1/_2$ cups	grated cheddar cheese
$^3/_4$ cup	sour cream
$^1/_2$ teaspoon	black pepper
1	refrigerated pie crust

Preheat oven to 425 degrees.

Spread broccoli into bottom of a lightly greased and micro-waveable 10-inch deep-dish pie pan or 1$^1/_2$-quart round dish.

In a bowl, mix corn, soup, ham, cheese, sour cream, and pepper together. Spoon mixture over broccoli. Cover with a paper towel and microwave on high heat 3–4$^1/_2$ minutes, or until hot. Place unfolded pie crust over ham mixture and tuck edges inside pan. Cut four 1-inch slits in crust to allow steam to escape during baking. Place pan on top of a baking sheet. Bake 15 minutes, or until crust turns golden brown.

Cheddar and Ham Noodle Casserole

MAKES 4–6 SERVINGS

1 bag (12 ounces)	egg noodles
¼ cup	diced green bell pepper
½	medium onion
1 tablespoon	olive oil
1 can (10.75 ounces)	condensed cream of mushroom soup
⅔ cup	milk
1½ cups	diced fully cooked ham
2 cups	grated cheddar cheese

Preheat oven to 400 degrees.

Cook noodles according to package directions and drain.

In a frying pan, sauté bell pepper and onion in olive oil until onion is translucent. Stir soup, milk, ham, vegetables, and cheese into warm noodles. Spread noodle mixture into a greased 2-quart baking dish. Bake 15 minutes, or until heated through.

Chicago-Style Pizza Casserole

MAKES 6–8 SERVINGS

2 tubes (13.8 ounces each)	**refrigerated pizza crust dough**
2 cups	**traditional spaghetti sauce, divided**
1 pound	**sausage, browned and drained**
1/2	**medium onion, chopped**
2 cups	**grated mozzarella cheese, divided**

Preheat oven to 375 degrees.

Spread 1 crust over bottom and up the sides of a lightly greased 9 x 13-inch pan. Spread 1½ cups sauce over crust. Spread cooked sausage and onion over sauce. Sprinkle 1½ cups cheese over sausage layer.

Place remaining pizza crust over top and pinch dough from the lower and upper crusts together. Cut 1-inch slits in top crust. Carefully spread remaining sauce and cheese over top.

Bake 30 minutes, or until crust is golden brown and done in the center.

Country Broccoli, Cheese, and Ham

MAKES 4–6 SERVINGS

1 package (10 ounces)	frozen broccoli
1 cup	diced fully cooked ham
1 can (10.75 ounces)	condensed cheddar cheese soup
½ cup	sour cream
2 cups	breadcrumbs
1 tablespoon	butter or margarine, melted

Preheat oven to 350 degrees.

Cook broccoli according to package directions. In a large bowl, combine broccoli, ham, soup, and sour cream. Transfer mixture into a greased 9 x 13-inch pan. In a medium bowl, combine breadcrumbs and butter, and then sprinkle over mixture. Bake 30–35 minutes.

Ham-and-Swiss Pork Chops

MAKES 4–6 SERVINGS

6	pork chops
1 tablespoon	butter or margarine
12	fresh bay leaves
6	slices ham
2 tablespoons	chopped fresh sage
1 cup	grated Swiss cheese

Preheat oven to 375 degrees.

In a frying pan, brown pork chops in butter 2–3 minutes on each side. Set on a plate lined with paper towels to drain.

In a greased 9 x 13-inch pan, layer pork chops, bay leaves, ham, sage, and cheese. Cover and bake 25 minutes.

Hash Brown Heaven

MAKES 6–8 SERVINGS

4 cups	**frozen shredded hash browns, thawed**
1 pound	**bacon, cooked and crumbled**
2/3 cup	**milk**
1/2 cup	**chopped onion**
1/2 teaspoon	**salt**
1/4 teaspoon	**black pepper**
1/8 teaspoon	**garlic powder (optional)**
2 tablespoons	**butter or margarine, melted**

Preheat oven to 350 degrees.

Combine hash browns, bacon, milk, onion, salt, pepper, garlic powder, if using, and butter in a large bowl. Transfer to a greased 8 x 8-inch pan. Bake 45 minutes.

Make it cheesy by sprinkling 1 cup grated cheddar cheese over casserole immediately after baking.

Jambalaya

MAKES 6–8 SERVINGS

½ cup	butter or margarine
1	large onion, chopped
1	large green bell pepper, chopped
½ cup	diced celery
1 tablespoon	minced garlic
1 pound	fully cooked smoked sausage links, cut into ½-inch slices
3 cups	chicken broth
2 cups	uncooked white rice
1 cup	chopped tomatoes
½ cup	chopped green onion
1½ tablespoons	parsley
1 tablespoon	Worcestershire sauce
1 tablespoon	Tabasco sauce

Preheat oven to 375 degrees.

In a frying pan, melt butter. Sauté onion, bell pepper, celery, and garlic in butter until tender.

In a large bowl, combine sausage, broth, rice, tomatoes, green onion, parsley, Worcestershire sauce, and Tabasco sauce. Stir sautéed vegetables into sausage mixture. Spread into a greased 9 x 13-inch pan. Cover and bake 20 minutes. Stir, cover, and bake 20 minutes more. Stir, cover, and bake a final 5–10 minutes, or until rice is done.

Orange Rice and Pork Chops

MAKES 6 SERVINGS

6	**pork chops**
	salt and pepper, to taste
1⅓ cups	**uncooked white rice**
1 cup	**orange juice**
1 can (10.75 ounces)	**condensed chicken and rice soup**

Preheat oven to 350 degrees.

In a frying pan, brown pork chops 2 minutes on each side and season with salt and pepper. Set aside.

In a greased 9 x 13-inch pan, combine rice and orange juice. Place pork chops over rice. Pour soup over top. Cover and bake 45 minutes. Uncover and cook 10 minutes more, or until done.

Sausage and Pepperoni Casserole

MAKES 4–6 SERVINGS

1 pound	sausage
1	medium onion, chopped
1 package (3.5 ounces)	sliced pepperoni
1 jar (14 ounces)	pizza sauce
1¼ cups	grated mozzarella cheese
1 cup	biscuit mix
1 cup	milk
2	eggs, lightly beaten

Preheat oven to 400 degrees.

In a frying pan, brown sausage and onion together until sausage is done. Drain any excess grease then stir in pepperoni. Spread meat mixture into a greased 8 x 8-inch pan. Pour pizza sauce evenly over meat. Sprinkle cheese over sauce.

In a separate bowl, mix biscuit mix, milk, and eggs together. Pour batter evenly over meat mixture and sauce. Bake, uncovered, 25 minutes, or until golden brown.

BEEF

Rotini Bake

MAKES 6–8 SERVINGS

12 ounces	uncooked curly rotini or small tube pasta
1 pound	ground beef
1 jar (26 ounces)	spaghetti sauce
2	eggs, slightly beaten
1 carton (16 ounces)	cottage cheese
2 cups	grated mozzarella cheese, divided
½ cup	grated Parmesan cheese

Preheat oven to 350 degrees.

Cook noodles according to package directions and drain.

In a frying pan, brown and drain beef while noodles cook. Stir spaghetti sauce into beef.

In a large bowl, combine eggs, cottage cheese, 1 cup mozzarella cheese, and Parmesan cheese. Gently fold cooked pasta into cheese mixture. Spread a third of beef mixture over bottom of a greased 9 x 13-inch pan. Place half the pasta mixture over beef. Layer another third of beef mixture over noodles. Layer remaining noodles over top, followed by remaining beef mixture.

Cover and bake 40 minutes. Uncover and sprinkle remaining mozzarella cheese over top. Return to oven and bake 5–10 minutes more, or until cheese is melted.

Beef Potpie

MAKES 6–8 SERVINGS

1 pound	**lean beef stew meat, cooked**
1 package (16 ounces)	**frozen mixed vegetables, thawed**
1 jar (12 ounces)	**mushroom gravy**
½ teaspoon	**thyme**
1 tube (8 ounces)	**refrigerated crescent rolls**

Preheat oven to 375 degrees.

Combine beef, vegetables, gravy, and thyme in a greased 9 x 13-inch pan. Bake 20 minutes. Remove from oven and place flattened dough over top. Return to oven and bake 17–19 minutes, or until crust is golden brown.

Cornbread on Chili

MAKES 6–8 SERVINGS

1	medium onion, chopped
1 tablespoon	butter or margarine
2 cans (15 ounces each)	chili with meat and beans
1 can (11 ounces)	Mexican-style corn, drained
1 cup	grated cheddar cheese
1 package	cornbread mix (8 x 8-inch pan size)

Preheat oven to 425 degrees.

In a frying pan, sauté onion in butter until tender. Stir in chili and corn. Spread chili mixture into a greased 9 x 13-inch pan. Sprinkle cheese over top.

In a bowl, mix cornbread mix according to package directions. Pour batter evenly over chili mixture. Bake 25 minutes, or until cornbread is golden brown and set in the center.

Enchilada Casserole

MAKES 6 SERVINGS

1 pound	ground beef, browned and drained
1 can (15 ounces)	chili, any variety
1 can (8 ounces)	tomato sauce
1 can (10 ounces)	enchilada sauce
1 bag (10 ounces)	corn chips, divided
1 cup	sour cream
1 cup	grated cheddar cheese

Preheat oven to 350 degrees.

In a large bowl, combine cooked beef, chili, tomato sauce, and enchilada sauce. Stir in two-thirds of the chips. Spread mixture into a greased 2-quart baking dish. Bake, uncovered, 24–28 minutes, or until heated through.

Spread sour cream over top. Sprinkle cheese over sour cream. Crush remaining chips and sprinkle over top. Bake 5–8 minutes more, or until cheese is melted.

Cream Cheese Enchiladas

MAKES 6–8 SERVINGS

1 pound	**ground beef, browned and drained**
½ cup	**chopped onion**
2 cans (8 ounces each)	**tomato sauce**
¼ cup	**water**
1½ teaspoons	**chili powder**
½ teaspoon	**black pepper**
1 package (8 ounces)	**cream cheese, softened**
12	**medium flour tortillas**
2 cups	**grated cheddar cheese**
	shredded lettuce, for serving
	sour cream, for serving

Preheat oven to 375 degrees.

In a large bowl, combine cooked beef, onion, tomato sauce, water, and spices. Spread cream cheese over tortillas, roll up, and place in a greased 9 x 13-inch pan. Pour beef mixture over tortillas. Sprinkle with cheddar cheese. Cover and bake 25 minutes. Serve over shredded lettuce and top with a dollop of sour cream.

Chilighetti

MAKES 6–8 SERVINGS

1 pound	**ground beef, browned and drained**
1 package (8 ounces)	**spaghetti, cooked and drained**
½ cup	**chopped onion**
1 cup	**sour cream**
2 cans (8 ounces each)	**tomato sauce**
1 can (4 ounces)	**sliced mushrooms**
2 cans (16 ounces each)	**chili, any type**
1 clove	**garlic, minced**
2 cups	**grated cheddar cheese**

Preheat oven to 350 degrees.

In a large bowl, combine all ingredients except cheese. Transfer mixture into a greased 9 x 13-inch pan. Top with cheese. Bake 20 minutes.

Deep-Dish Tacos

MAKES 4 SERVINGS

½ cup	sour cream
½ cup	mayonnaise
½ cup	grated cheddar cheese
¼ cup	chopped onion
1 cup	biscuit mix
¼ cup	cold water
½ pound	ground beef, browned and drained
1	medium tomato, thinly sliced
½ cup	green bell pepper, chopped

Preheat oven to 375 degrees.

In a bowl, combine sour cream, mayonnaise, cheese, and onion. Set aside.

In a separate bowl, mix biscuit mix and water until a soft dough forms. Press dough on bottom and up the sides of a greased 8 x 8-inch pan. Layer beef, tomato, and bell pepper over dough. Spoon sour cream mixture over top. Bake 25–30 minutes.

Cowboy Casserole

MAKES 6–8 SERVINGS

1 pound	ground beef
1	medium onion, chopped
2	jalapeño peppers, seeded and diced
2 packages (6.5 ounces each)	cornbread mix
½ teaspoon	salt
½ teaspoon	baking soda
1 can (14.75 ounces)	cream-style corn
¾ cup	milk
2	eggs, beaten
2 cups	grated cheddar cheese, divided

Preheat oven to 350 degrees.

In a frying pan, brown beef with onion and peppers until beef is done. Drain any excess grease and set aside.

In a bowl, combine cornbread mix, salt, baking soda, corn, milk, and eggs.

Spread half the batter over bottom of a greased 9 x 13-inch pan. Sprinkle half the cheese over batter. Spoon meat mixture evenly over top. Sprinkle remaining cheese over meat mixture, and then spread remaining batter over top. Bake, uncovered, 35 minutes, or until cornbread is golden brown and set in the center.

Incredible Cheeseburger Pie

MAKES 4 SERVINGS

1 pound	ground beef, browned and drained
1 cup	chopped onion
1 cup	grated cheddar cheese
1 cup	milk
½ cup	biscuit mix
2	eggs

Preheat oven to 325 degrees.

In a greased 9 x 9-inch pan, layer beef, onion, and cheese.

In a bowl, combine milk, biscuit mix, and eggs. Spread dough mixture over cheese. Bake 25–35 minutes, or until knife inserted in the center comes out clean.

Italian Macaroni Bake

MAKES 6 SERVINGS

8 ounces	**uncooked elbow macaroni**
1 pound	**ground beef, browned and drained, divided**
	salt and pepper, to taste
1 jar (14 ounces)	**pizza sauce, divided**
1 can (4 ounces)	**sliced mushrooms, divided**
2 cups	**grated mozzarella cheese, divided**

Preheat oven to 350 degrees.

Cook macaroni according to package directions and drain.

Season cooked beef with salt and pepper. Place half the macaroni into bottom of a greased 2-quart baking dish. Layer half each of the beef, pizza sauce, mushrooms, and cheese. Place remaining macaroni over top and repeat layers. Cover and bake 20 minutes. Uncover and bake 5–10 minutes more, or until cheese is melted.

Meat and Potato Casserole

MAKES 6–8 SERVINGS

1 pound	ground beef
2	medium onions, chopped
1½ teaspoons	Italian seasoning
4 to 6	medium potatoes, peeled and thinly sliced
	salt and pepper, to taste
1 can (10.75 ounces)	condensed cream of mushroom soup
⅓ cup	water

Preheat oven to 350 degrees.

In a frying pan, brown beef and onions together until beef is done. Stir Italian seasoning into beef mixture.

Lay a third of the potatoes on bottom of a greased 9 x 13-inch pan. Sprinkle potatoes with salt and pepper. Spread half the beef mixture over top. Repeat layers, ending with potato layer. Combine soup and water. Spread soup mixture over top. Cover and bake 1 hour.

Meatball Casserole

MAKES 6–8 SERVINGS

1 can (10.75 ounces)	condensed cream of chicken soup
1 cup	sour cream
1 cup	grated cheddar cheese
1	large onion, chopped
1 teaspoon	salt
1 teaspoon	black pepper
1 package (30 ounces)	frozen shredded hash browns, thawed
20	precooked frozen meatballs

Preheat oven to 350 degrees.

In a bowl, stir together soup, sour cream, cheese, onion, salt, and pepper. With a paper towel, pat hash browns dry and then stir into soup mixture. Spread hash brown mixture into a greased 9 x 13-inch pan. Slightly press meatballs into hash brown mixture in even rows. Cover and bake 35 minutes. Uncover and bake 10–15 minutes more, or until hash browns are done.

Onion Ring Barbecue Bake

MAKES 6–8 SERVINGS

1½ pounds	ground beef
1	medium onion, chopped
1 jar (18 ounces)	hickory barbecue sauce
1 bag (16 ounces)	frozen onion rings

Preheat oven to 425 degrees.

In a frying pan, brown beef and onion together until beef is done. Drain any excess grease. Stir barbecue sauce into beef and onion. Spread beef mixture into a greased 9 x 13-inch pan. Place onion rings evenly over top. Bake 20–25 minutes, or until onion rings are crisp.

#81

Pizza Puffs

MAKES 6–8 SERVINGS

1 pound	**ground beef, browned and drained**
1 can (15 ounces)	**pizza sauce**
2 tubes (7.5 ounces each)	**refrigerated biscuits**
2 cups	**grated mozzarella cheese**
½ cup	**grated cheddar cheese**

Preheat oven to 400 degrees.

In a bowl, combine cooked beef and pizza sauce. Cut biscuits into 4 pieces each and place in a greased 9 x 13-inch pan. Pour beef mixture over top. Bake, uncovered, 20–25 minutes. Sprinkle cheese over top. Bake 3–7 minutes more, or until cheese is melted.

Sloppy Joe Pie

MAKES 4–6 SERVINGS

1 pound	ground beef
1	medium onion, chopped
1 can (15 ounces)	crushed tomatoes, with liquid
1 envelope	sloppy joe seasoning
1 tube (8 ounces)	refrigerated crescent roll dough

Preheat oven to 375 degrees.

In a frying pan, brown beef and onion together until beef is done. Stir crushed tomatoes and seasoning into beef and onion. Simmer over medium-low heat 5 minutes, stirring occasionally.

Place beef mixture into a greased, deep 9-inch pie pan or round baking dish.

Lay individually flattened crescents over top, placing the skinny point in the center, stretching the bottom edge of the crescent dough triangle to the outside of the pan. Overlap dough if necessary. Bake 15 minutes, or until crust is golden brown.

Southwest Casserole

MAKES 6–8 SERVINGS

1 pound	ground beef, browned and drained
2 cans (8 ounces each)	tomato sauce
1 can (12–15 ounces)	whole-kernel corn, drained
1 envelope	taco seasoning
10	medium gordita-style flour tortillas
1 can (10.75 ounces)	condensed cream of celery soup
3/4 cup	milk
1 1/2 cups	grated cheddar or Mexican-blend cheese

Preheat oven to 350 degrees.

In a bowl, combine cooked beef, tomato sauce, corn, and taco seasoning.

Use 6 tortillas to cover bottom and sides of a greased 9 x 13-inch pan. Spread beef mixture over tortillas. Use remaining tortillas to cover beef mixture, cutting to fit if necessary.

In a bowl, mix together soup and milk and pour over tortillas. Sprinkle cheese over top. Bake 20–25 minutes, or until edges turn golden brown.

Tater Tot Casserole

MAKES 6–8 SERVINGS

1 pound	ground beef
1	medium onion, chopped
2 cans (10.75 ounces each)	condensed cream of mushroom or cream of chicken soup
1 can (14.5 ounces)	whole-kernel corn, drained
1 cup	grated cheddar cheese
1 package (27–32 ounces)	frozen tater tots

Preheat oven to 350 degrees.

In a frying pan, brown beef and onion together until beef is done. Drain any excess grease. Place beef mixture into bottom of a greased 9 x 13-inch pan. Spoon 1 can soup over top. Sprinkle corn and cheese over soup layer. Cover with tater tots, laying tater tots on their sides. Spread remaining can of soup over tater tots. Bake 40 minutes.

FAMILY FAVORITES

Buried Pepperoni Supreme Pizza

MAKES 6–8 SERVINGS

2 tubes (13.8 ounces)	refrigerated pizza crust dough
2 cans (8 ounces each)	tomato sauce, divided
1 teaspoon	Italian seasoning
24	pepperoni slices
1 can (4 ounces)	mushroom pieces, drained
1 can (3.8 ounces)	sliced olives, drained
2 cups	grated mozzarella cheese, divided

Preheat oven to 375 degrees.

Spread 1 crust over bottom and up the sides of a lightly greased 9 x 13-inch pan. Spread 1½ cans tomato sauce over bottom crust. Sprinkle Italian seasoning over sauce, and then layer pepperoni, mushrooms, and olives over top. Sprinkle 1½ cups cheese over pepperoni layer.

Place remaining pizza crust over top. Pinch the lower and upper dough crust together. Cut four 1-inch slits in top of crust. Spread remaining sauce and cheese over top. Bake 30 minutes, or until crust is golden brown and done in the center.

Deep-Dish Sausage Pizza

MAKES 6–8 SERVINGS

1 tube (13.8 ounces)	refrigerated pizza crust dough
1 can (8 ounces)	tomato sauce
1½ teaspoons	Italian seasoning
1 pound	sausage, browned and drained
1 can (3.8 ounces)	sliced olives, drained
½	onion, thinly sliced
⅓ cup	chopped green bell pepper
1½ cups	grated mozzarella cheese

Preheat oven to 425 degrees.

Press dough over bottom and halfway up the sides of a lightly greased 9 x 13-inch pan. Bake 9 minutes. Spread tomato sauce over crust. Sprinkle Italian seasoning and cooked sausage over sauce. Layer olives, onion, and bell pepper over sausage and then sprinkle cheese over top. Bake 7–11 minutes, or until cheese is melted and crust is golden brown.

Easy Lasagna

MAKES 8 SERVINGS

1	egg, beaten
¼ cup	grated Parmesan cheese
1½ teaspoons	Italian seasoning
1 container (16 ounces)	cottage cheese, divided
2 cups	grated mozzarella cheese, divided
1 pound	ground beef
1	medium onion, chopped
½ cup	water
2 cans (26 ounces each)	chunky spaghetti sauce, divided
1 box (12 ounces)	uncooked oven-ready lasagna noodles

Preheat oven to 350 degrees.

In a bowl, combine egg, Parmesan, Italian seasoning, cottage cheese, and 1 cup mozzarella cheese. Set aside.

In a large frying pan, brown beef and onion together until beef is done. Drain any excess grease. Add water and all but 1 cup of spaghetti sauce to beef. Spread reserved spaghetti sauce into bottom of a greased 9 x 13-inch pan. Layer 5–6 lasagna noodles over sauce, overlapping or breaking to fit, if necessary. Spread half the cheese mixture over noodles. Spoon a third of the beef mixture over cheese layer. Repeat layers once. Add one more layer of 5–6 noodles and spoon remaining third of beef mixture over top. Cover and bake 50 minutes. Sprinkle remaining mozzarella cheese over top. Let stand 5 minutes before serving.

Chilean-Inspired Corn Casserole

MAKES 6–8 SERVINGS

4 cans (15 ounces each)	whole-kernel corn, drained
1½ teaspoons	basil
1 teaspoon	salt
3 tablespoons	butter or margarine
1 tablespoon	cornstarch
1½ pounds	ground beef
3	large onions, chopped
1 teaspoon	ground cumin
1 can (2.25 ounces)	sliced black olives, drained
½ cup	raisins
2 tablespoons	sugar

Preheat oven to 400 degrees.

In a blender, grind corn for 3 minutes. Pour liquefied corn into a saucepan with basil, salt, and butter. Heat until it starts to bubble. Slowly stir in cornstarch to thicken.

In a frying pan, brown beef and onions together. Drain any excess grease. Stir cumin into beef mixture. Spoon beef mixture into bottom of a greased 9 x 13-inch pan. Sprinkle olives and raisins over beef mixture. Spread corn mixture evenly over top. Sprinkle sugar over corn layer. Bake 40–50 minutes, or until golden brown.

The traditional Chilean dish, *pastel de choclo*, is often served with a side of sugar.

Baked Mostaccioli

MAKES 6–8 SERVINGS

1 pound	**ground beef, cooked and drained**
1½ jars (26 ounces each)	**spaghetti sauce**
1 package (12 ounces)	**mostaccioli noodles**
2 cups	**grated mozzarella cheese**
⅓ cup	**grated Parmesan cheese**

Preheat oven to 350 degrees. Combine beef and spaghetti sauce. Set aside.

Cook noodles according to package directions and drain. In a greased 9 x 13-inch pan, layer half each of the pasta, beef mixture, and mozzarella cheese. Repeat layers, and then top with Parmesan. Cover and bake 40 minutes. Uncover and cook 10 minutes more.

Mac and Cheese Bake

MAKES 4–6 SERVINGS

3 cups	**uncooked elbow macaroni**
1 jar (16 ounces)	**cheddar cheese sauce, such as Ragu Double Cheddar**
1	**green onion, chopped (optional)**
¼ cup	**seasoned breadcrumbs**

Preheat oven to 400 degrees.

Cook macaroni according to package directions and drain. Stir in cheddar sauce, and green onion, if desired. Spread macaroni mixture into a greased 2-quart baking dish. Sprinkle breadcrumbs over top. Cover and bake 12–15 minutes. Uncover and bake 5 minutes more.

Fish and Cheesy Pasta Casserole

MAKES 5 SERVINGS

16 ounces	**curly pasta, cooked and drained**
1 jar (16 ounces)	**cheddar cheese sauce, such as Ragu Double Cheddar**
5	**frozen battered fish fillets**

Preheat oven to 375 degrees.

Cook pasta according to package directions and drain. Place pasta into a greased 9 x 13-inch pan. Stir cheddar sauce into noodles. Place fish over top. Bake, uncovered, 30 minutes.

#92

Home-Style Shells and Cheese

MAKES 6 SERVINGS

1 package (16 ounces)	**small shell pasta**
1 can (10.75 ounces)	**condensed tomato soup**
1½ cups	**grated cheddar cheese, divided**

Preheat oven to 350 degrees.

Cook shells according to package directions and drain. Stir soup and 1 cup cheddar cheese into shells. Spread mixture into a greased 9 x 13-inch pan. Sprinkle remaining cheese over top. Bake 25–30 minutes.

Cheeseburger Casserole

MAKES 6–8 SERVINGS

2 pounds	ground beef
1	large onion, chopped
1 teaspoon	salt
½ teaspoon	black pepper
1¾ cups	grated cheddar cheese
1 cup	biscuit mix
1¾ cups	milk
3	eggs, lightly beaten

Preheat oven to 400 degrees.

Brown beef and onion together in a large frying pan. Drain any excess grease. Stir salt and pepper into beef and onion. Spread mixture into a greased 9 x 13-inch pan. Sprinkle cheese over top.

In a bowl, mix together biscuit mix, milk, and eggs. Pour batter over top. Bake 25–30 minutes, or until lightly golden brown and set in the center.

Chicken Rice

MAKES 6–8 SERVINGS

1	green bell pepper, chopped
1	medium onion, chopped
1 cup	uncooked white rice
½ cup	butter or margarine
2 cans (10.75 ounces each)	condensed chicken and rice soup
1 cup	water

Preheat oven to 350 degrees.

In a frying pan, sauté bell pepper, onion, and rice in butter about 5 minutes.

In a greased 9 x 13-inch pan, combine rice mixture, soup, and water. Cover and bake 45–55 minutes.

Baked Beans 'n' Dogs

MAKES 6–8 SERVINGS

3 cans (15.5 ounces each)	**pork and beans**
1 package (8–10 count)	**hot dogs, sliced**
½ cup	**brown sugar**
¼ cup	**ketchup**
¼ cup	**dried minced onion**
2 teaspoons	**mustard**

Preheat oven to 350 degrees.

Mix pork and beans, hot dogs, brown sugar, ketchup, onion, and mustard together in a 2- to 3-quart baking dish. Bake, uncovered, 45 minutes, or until bubbly.

Quick Sloppy Joe Potpie

MAKES 4–6 SERVINGS

1 pound	**ground beef, browned and drained**
1 can (15.5 ounces)	**sloppy joe sauce**
1 can (11 ounces)	**Mexican-style corn**
2 cups	**grated cheddar cheese**
1 tube (6 ounces)	**refrigerated biscuits**

Preheat oven to 375 degrees.

Combine cooked beef, sloppy joe sauce, and corn.

Layer beef mixture in the bottom of a 9 x 9-inch pan. Sprinkle cheese over top. Cut biscuits in half and lay over cheese, cut side down. Bake 15–20 minutes.

Taco Pie

MAKES 6 SERVINGS

1 tube (8 ounces)	refrigerated crescent roll dough
1½ pounds	ground beef
1	medium onion, chopped
1 envelope	taco seasoning
1 cup	salsa
1½ cups	grated Mexican-blend cheese
1 bag (10 ounces)	shredded lettuce
2	Roma tomatoes, diced
2 cups	crushed nacho cheese tortilla chips

Preheat oven to 350 degrees.

Cover bottom of a greased 9 x 13-inch pan with crescent dough. Bake 10–14 minutes, or until light golden brown.

In a frying pan, brown beef and onion together until beef is done. Drain any excess grease. Stir taco seasoning and salsa into beef. Spread beef mixture over baked crust. Sprinkle cheese over top. Bake 2–5 minutes, or until cheese is melted. Layer lettuce, tomatoes, and crushed chips over top. Serve immediately.

Stuffed Pasta Shells

MAKES 6 SERVINGS

1 package (12 ounces)	**large pasta shells**
1 container (16 ounces)	**cottage cheese**
1	**egg, slightly beaten**
2 cups	**grated mozzarella cheese**
1 jar (26 ounces)	**spaghetti sauce**

Preheat oven to 350 degrees.

Cook shells according to package directions and drain.

In a bowl, combine cottage cheese, egg, and mozzarella. Stuff cooked shells with cheese mixture. Place shells in a lightly greased 9 x 13-inch pan. Pour spaghetti sauce over shells. Cover and bake 45 minutes, or until sauce is bubbly.

Chili Casserole

MAKES 6 SERVINGS

1 bag (14 ounces)	**tortilla chips, crushed**
2 cans (15 ounces each)	**chili con carne**
1 can (8 ounces)	**tomato sauce**
2 cups	**grated cheddar cheese**

Preheat oven to 350 degrees.

Sprinkle half the chips over bottom of a glass 9 x 13-inch pan. Spread 1 can chili over chip layer. Drizzle half the tomato sauce over top. Sprinkle 1 cup cheese over sauce. Repeat layers. Bake 17–22 minutes. Serve with salsa on the side.

Tuna–Tater Tot Casserole

MAKES 6 SERVINGS

1 package (32 ounces)	**frozen tater tots**
1 can (6 ounces)	**tuna, drained**
1 can (10.75 ounces)	**condensed cream of chicken soup**
½ cup	**milk**
1½ cups	**grated cheddar cheese**

Preheat oven to 350 degrees.

Place tater tots in a greased 2-quart baking dish. Combine tuna, soup, and milk. Pour over tater tots and then sprinkle with cheese. Cover and bake 1 hour.

Canned chicken or ham may be substituted.

Traditional Tuna Casserole

MAKES 4–6 SERVINGS

1 bag (12 ounces)	**egg noodles**
1 can (10.75 ounces)	**condensed cream of mushroom soup**
½ cup	**milk**
1 can (6 ounces)	**tuna, drained**
2 cups	**grated cheddar cheese**
½ cup	**crushed cheddar and sour cream potato chips**

Preheat oven to 400 degrees.

Cook noodles according to package directions and drain. Stir soup, milk, tuna, and cheese into noodles. Spread noodle mixture into a greased 2-quart baking dish. Bake 15 minutes. Top with crushed chips and bake 3–5 minutes more.

Add 1 cup cooked peas to the noodle mixture before baking.

NOTES

NOTES

NOTES

NOTES

NOTES

NOTES

NOTES

Metric Conversion Chart

VOLUME MEASUREMENTS

U.S.	Metric
1 teaspoon	5 ml
1 tablespoon	15 ml
¼ cup	60 ml
⅓ cup	75 ml
½ cup	125 ml
⅔ cup	150 ml
¾ cup	175 ml
1 cup	250 ml

WEIGHT MEASUREMENTS

U.S.	Metric
½ ounce	15 g
1 ounce	30 g
3 ounces	90 g
4 ounces	115 g
8 ounces	225 g
12 ounces	350 g
1 pound	450 g
2¼ pounds	1 kg

TEMPERATURE CONVERSION

Fahrenheit	Celsius
250	120
300	150
325	160
350	180
375	190
400	200
425	220
450	230

MORE 101 THINGS® IN THESE
FAVORITES

BACON
CAKE MIX
RAMEN NOODLES
SLOW COOKER
SMOKER

Each 128 pages, $12.99

Available at bookstores or directly from Gibbs Smith
1.800.835.4993
www.gibbs-smith.com

Gibbs Smith

About the Authors

Stephanie Ashcraft was raised in Indiana. She received a bachelor's degree in family science and a teaching certificate from Brigham Young University. Stephanie loves teaching, interacting with people, and spending time with friends and family. She has taught hundreds of classes and appeared on hundreds of television and news programs all over the country sharing ways families can save time and money in the kitchen. Stephanie and her husband, Ivan, reside in Salem, Utah, with their five children.

Janet Eyring, a cooking instructor, is the author of four cookbooks and lives in Heber, Utah.